LITTLE LOOM
WEAVING

Quick and Clever Projects for Creating Adorable Stuff

ANDREIA GOMES

Ulysses Press

Published in the U.S. by

Ulysses Press
P.O. Box 3440
Berkeley, CA 94703
www.ulyssespress.com

ISBN: 978-1-61243-663-0
Library of Congress Control Number 2016957526

Printed in the United States by Bang Printing
10 9 8 7 6 5 4 3 2 1

Acquisitions editor: Casie Vogel
Managing editor: Claire Chun
Project Editor: Shayna Keyles
Editor: Renee Rutledge
Cover design: Michelle Thompson
Interior design and layout: what!design @ whatweb.com
Artwork: © Andreia Gomes except color wheel page 18 © Plateresca/Shutterstock.com; author photo page 111 © Pedro Pereira

Distributed by Publishers Group West

CONTENTS

INTRODUCTION

With a background in interior design, I am naturally drawn to textiles and art. I have always appreciated the process of creating things with my own hands. I'm someone who is creative and has experimented with all kinds of crafts, from sewing to macrame to upcycling. Call me a compulsive maker.

A few years ago, I discovered the world of weaving. I was intrigued by the beauty of it, and almost immediately, I wanted to learn. I started teaching myself by reading tutorials in old magazines and vintage books. My very first weave was done on a cardboard loom. It started out as a hobby, but then I realized I wanted to do it more and more—I was addicted! That was when I decided to buy my first "real" loom, and I have not looked back since.

Over the past few years, I have fallen in love with fiber arts, especially weaving. I enjoy the entire process of choosing fibers and colors, imagining dozens of new designs at the same time. It's amazing to be able to create what I imagine and see it take shape.

Weaving can be a relaxing and meditative process, as well as a fun and rewarding one. The time I spend on the loom is time away from my everyday problems and concerns; it helps clear my mind, and afterward, I feel a sense of peace and satisfaction.

In recent years, weaving has seen a revival as a modern craft. Artisans and crafters are bringing this ancient art back and keeping the skills and traditions alive. I see more and more people interested in this art and getting involved in the growing community of weavers.

When I started weaving, there were almost no tutorials available, so I had to learn on my own, and it took me a long time before I created a piece that I was proud of. That was one of the reasons why I wanted to write this book.

I want to share with you what I've learned through my experience and help you start your creative journey. With this book, you will not only learn the foundational skills, but also will be able to create your own projects, making this book a source for both beginners and more advanced weavers.

This book is meant for everyone who wants to learn the fascinating art of weaving in a simple, fun, and modern way. Within these pages, I will show you the basic skills necessary to get you started on weaving.

First, I'll introduce you to the materials, tools, and types of fibers you need to recognize before you start. Then, I will guide you through the whole process, from warping your loom to finishing your piece, with a selection of basic techniques. You will learn how to create shapes and how to add texture to your piece using rya knots or loops; plus, you'll find a few useful tips that I'm sure will make your work easier.

I also want to inspire you to create new things by showing the diversity of what you can make with your loom. This step-by-step guide includes 15 projects, from wall hangings, pillows, and other home decor objects, to wearable items like a necklace or bracelet, to repurposed objects such as a branch or a piece of driftwood.

More than just a collection of do-it-yourself projects, this book will push you out of your comfort zone and inspire you to continue creating in your own way.

I had so much fun working on all the projects for this book, and I really hope you enjoy learning and creating your own woven objects. Have fun with the process, embrace your mistakes, and keep going—it will help you to be better next time.

There is no limit to what you can make with a simple loom, yarn, and some creativity.

Ready, set, go!

Andreia

WEAVING LOOM AND TOOLS

Weaving is the art of forming a cloth by interlacing, at right angles, two distinct sets of yarn, the vertical and horizontal threads. It is one of the most ancient and fundamental arts in the world, dating from before 5,000 BC, with finger weaving, tying, and twisting being some of the first cloth-making techniques.

Weaving technology has evolved from the simple handloom, made with a basic wooden frame, to the high-tech electronic weaving machines of today. Machine weaving produces quantities of standardized material for our everyday use, but some of the finest silks, table linens, and carpets are still woven on traditional handlooms.

Cloth is usually woven on a loom, which is a device that holds the warp threads in place while the weft threads are woven through them. Several types of loom have been developed over the centuries, like the warp-weighted loom and backstrap loom (the early versions of a loom) to modern versions like the heddle loom and the flying shuttle loom that were invented in the eighteenth century.

These days, weaving has become a mechanized process; however, we can still find small weaving communities around the world making cloth on handlooms. In recent years, weaving has made a comeback as a modern craft. More and more artisans and crafters are keeping the skills and traditions alive.

In this book, I will focus on the artisanal and rustic process of handweaving, but with a modern approach.

When I started weaving, I came across many choices and had many doubts. What kind of loom is more suitable for me? Do I need a big and expensive loom to start? What tools do I really need?

It may be difficult for new weavers to know how to set priorities for what to buy, especially since weaving equipment can be expensive. A loom is only one of the things you will need. While there is a wide range of weaving equipment available, you won't need much to get started. However, knowing what is available is important, even if you don't feel the need to have it all right away.

In this chapter, you will learn more about looms and other useful tools before you start your weaving journey.

WEAVING LOOM

The basic purpose of any loom is to hold the warp under tension to facilitate the interweaving of the other yarn. There are a number of looms available on the market that range in size and feature, from the bigger and more expensive table and floor looms, to the rigid heddle or tapestry looms. The tapestry loom is easy to warp and weave, portable, and not very expensive, making it perfect for either a beginner or an experienced weaver. We will focus our study on the tapestry loom.

This tapestry loom, also called the frame loom, is available in small and large sizes. You can choose the size depending on what project you have in mind; the size of the loom will define the size of the projects you can create with it.

You can learn to weave using the simplest of looms. If you don't want to invest in a loom right away, you can create a simple frame loom following the instructions in this book (see page 40), or you can improvise a loom using a piece of cardboard, an old frame you don't use anymore, and other basic materials (for plenty of ideas, do a quick search on the Internet

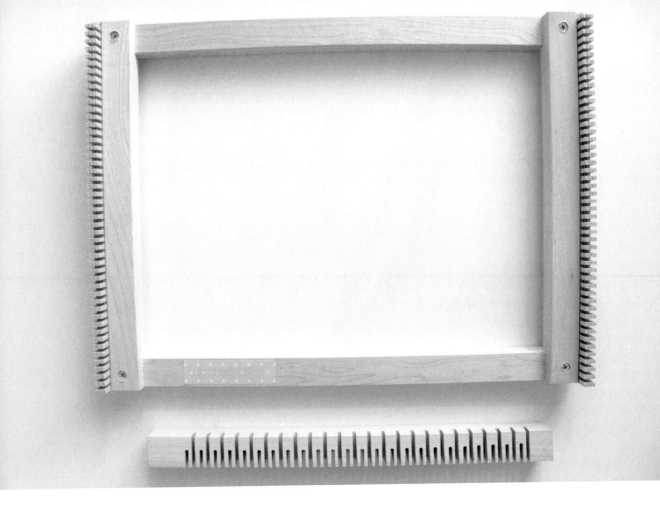

Weaving loom and rotating heddle bar.

for simple, do-it-yourself loom projects). Once you become addicted to weaving, you will likely want to upgrade to a more professional loom. There is a wide range of good quality, handcrafted looms, made with love and care, available on the market, and most of them are going to be worth the investment.

ESSENTIAL WEAVING TOOLS

The right tools will help you make the best use of your weaving materials and time. From my personal experience, when it comes to discovering essential weaving tools, nothing beats experimenting to see which ones work best for you. You'll find some tools very helpful and use them every time you weave; others, not so much. In this chapter, I've gathered some of the tools I think will make your weaving work easier and quicker.

Yarn and shuttle

LOOM: The equipment used to weave cloth and tapestry.

TAPESTRY NEEDLE: This is the most basic tool of weaving. It is a bigger needle that usually has a large eye to fit yarns with different thicknesses, and a bent tip to help you in the weaving process of going over and under the warp threads.

YARN NEEDLE: A longer needle with a round tip, this is a helpful tool when you have a bigger space to weave and want to save time.

TAPESTRY BEATER: The tapestry beater, also known as a fork or weaving comb, is a tool used to push the wefts together once you've woven them across the warp. These come in a variety of forms. When I started weaving and didn't have all the tools yet, I realized that using a hair comb would do almost the same job.

SHED STICK: The shed stick is a flat piece of wood used to separate the upper and lower warp yarns, creating a shed through which the weft is woven. This tool is very helpful and time saving when you are weaving large areas.

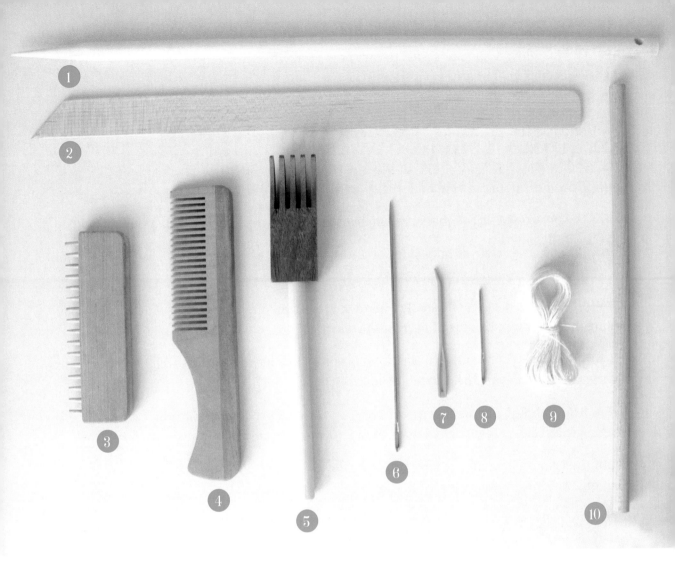

1. Wooden needle 2. Shed stick 3. Tapestry beater 4. Hair comb 5. Tapestry beater 6. Large needle 7. Tapestry needle 8. Yarn needle 9. Yarn 10. Wooden dowel.

HEDDLE: A heddle is a tool used to separate alternating warp threads, creating a shed. The main difference between a heddle and a shed stick is that with a heddle you can weave in both directions, rotating the heddle every time you need to change from one row to another.

SHUTTLE: A shuttle is a tool designed to carry the yarn when you are using a shed stick or a heddle to weave. Shuttles are passed back and forth through the shed, between the warp threads. The simplest shuttles are made from a flat piece of wood with notches on the ends to hold the weft yarn. Using this tool saves a lot of time when you are weaving one color across large areas.

TAPESTRY BOBBIN: A bobbin is used to carry the yarn while weaving. It is mostly used when you are weaving smaller areas in different colors.

WEAVING TERMS

WARP: The vertical thread held under tension on the loom during weaving.

WEFT: The horizontal thread that is woven over and under the warp threads to create cloth.

SELVAGE: The outer edge of both sides of a woven fabric that does not unravel because the weft yarns wrap around the warp yarns.

DRAW-IN: The act of unintentionally narrowing or tightening your selvage. It is caused by pulling the weft thread too tightly across the warp.

ARCHING: Pulling your weft yarn across your warp in order to make an arch while weaving each row. This will avoid the draw-in of your selvage.

BUBBLING: Pulling your weft yarn across your warp in order to make small curves while weaving each row. This will avoid the draw-in of your selvage.

SHED: The gap that occurs when you separate your warp threads into upper and lower positions. The opening/shed is for the weft thread to go through.

CLOTH: A piece of fabric formed by weaving, knitting, or felting from yarns made from materials such as wool, cotton, silk, nylon, or polyester.

PLY: An individual strand of yarn.

2

CHOOSING YARNS

When you enter a yarn shop, it's easy to be overwhelmed by all the choices in front of you. Yarn comes in all sorts of different shapes, sizes, colors, and textures. One of the things you need to have in mind before choosing the fibers you will use is what kind of piece you want to weave. Choosing the perfect yarn for a project is very important and can make all the difference in the finished piece. Choose the wrong yarn, and you can end up with a poorly executed or unfinished project.

Of course, this is not an easy thing to teach; you need a bit of practice to learn. The more you experiment weaving with different yarns, the more you will understand how they behave in different projects. If you are a beginner, I advise you to stick with wool and cotton in your first projects because they are easier to work with. As you improve your weaving skills, try as many yarns and textures as you want.

YARN FIBERS

Fibers are classified as natural or synthetic, depending on how they're sourced. Natural fibers, obtained from natural products, include animal and plant fibers like wool, cotton, silk, linen, and bamboo. Synthetic fibers, which are processed in machines, include acrylic, nylon, and polyester.

PLANT FIBERS

Plant fibers include cotton, linen, jute, bamboo, hemp, and sisal, among others. Plant fiber yarns can be a good choice if you are allergic to wool or lanolin. They are also the perfect choice if you are vegan.

COTTON: Cotton is obtained from the seeds of the cotton plant. It is the most widely used plant fiber, probably due to its softness and warmth. It is generally a lightweight fiber strong enough to be used for weaving.

LINEN: Linen is made from the fiber that comes from the flax plant. It is a strong and durable fiber. Flax has very little elasticity, so it can be tricky to weave with because it doesn't stretch much.

JUTE: The strongest and most affordable of all natural fibers, jute is the second most important plant fiber after cotton due to its versatility. It can be a little difficult for hand weavers to work with it.

BAMBOO: Environment-friendly bamboo is sometimes mixed with cotton or other raw materials. It has a silk-like sheen and the strength of cotton.

HEMP: Hemp is also known for its durability and strength, but it is softer fiber than jute.

SISAL: Sisal is a very stiff fiber, traditionally used for making rope and twine.

ANIMAL FIBERS

WOOL: Wool usually refers to the fleece from a sheep. It is the most common animal fiber and comes in a great variety of colors, textures, and styles, depending on its source. It is an easy fiber to work with because of its natural elasticity and the diversity of textures available on the market.

ALPACA: This is a very soft, silky, and beautiful yarn that comes from the South American animal named alpaca.

SILK: Silk is obtained from the cocoon of silkworm. Collected by hand, natural silk has been prized for centuries. It is known for its sheen, and unique and soft texture.

YARN WEIGHT

Yarn weight refers to the thickness of the yarn. Yarns are classified according to their thickness to help you choose the best one for each project. The Standard Yarn Weight System was created to categorize yarn weight in 7 different size designations. Each size, or weight, is assigned a name, starting with the thinnest and lightest type of yarn, lace, and ending with super bulky, a very thick yarn that is perfect for adding texture to your project.

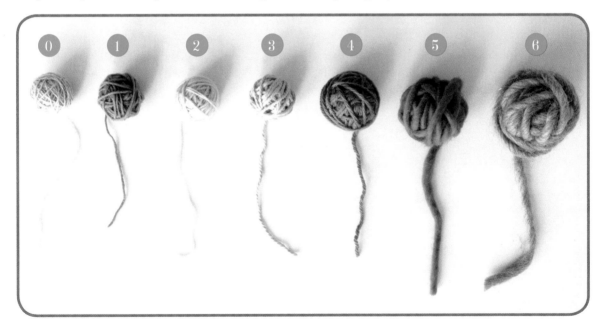

0: lace; 1: superfine; 2: fine; 3: light; 4: medium; 5: bulky; 6: super bulky

In this book, you will also see worsted weight yarns, which are usually light or medium weight yarns, and roving, which is a thick yarn that is larger than super bulky. For more on yarn weight and thickness, visit http://craftyarncouncil.com/weight.html.

COLOR THEORY: HOW TO CHOOSE COORDINATING COLORS OF YARNS

I believe most of us have, at least once, struggled to find the perfect color palette for a project. Working with color is not an exact science, but there are some color theories that can make your color-choosing process easier. One of them is using the basic color wheel. Many artists use the color wheel when creating their works of art.

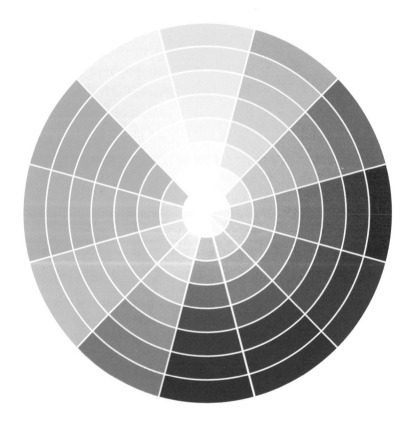

For a monochromatic look, choose one color and stick with it. Each color has multiple tones that can be mixed to create a color theme. If you are looking for a gradient effect, try to use three or more analogous colors. Analogous colors are any three colors that are side by side on the color wheel, like pink, red, and orange. If you want to make a project using complementary colors, choose colors directly across from each other on the color wheel, like orange and blue. Another important tip is to always add neutral colors to your weavings, like white, gray, or black.

CHOOSING A WARP YARN

The warp is the basis of every project. A warp yarn needs to be strong enough to hold up under the tension of the loom. The stronger your warp yarn is, the easier it will be to weave with it. A good way to test the strength of a yarn is to hold a piece of it with your hands and pull apart sharply. A strong warp yarn should remain intact and not break.

At the same time, a perfect warp has to be able to keep a uniform tension throughout the weaving process. This will keep your woven piece from shrinking on some edges when you take it off the loom.

In my opinion, the yarns that work best for warping are 100 percent cotton, due to cotton's strength and durability. My advice is that you start with a cotton yarn and experiment with other fibers as you feel more comfortable with weaving.

3

WEAVING
TECHNIQUES

In weaving, there are two essential elements that make the woven piece: the warp and the weft. The vertical threads are called the warp, and the horizontal threads are called the weft. Weaving weft over warp creates a strong, yet flexible structure that holds the individual threads in place, creating a solid cloth or fabric.

Learning the foundational skills of weaving is essential before you start your creative journey through this fiber art. The techniques and methods explained in this chapter are both simple and intuitive, and will allow you to make all kinds of projects with your loom, such as decorative wall hangings, rugs, or pillows.

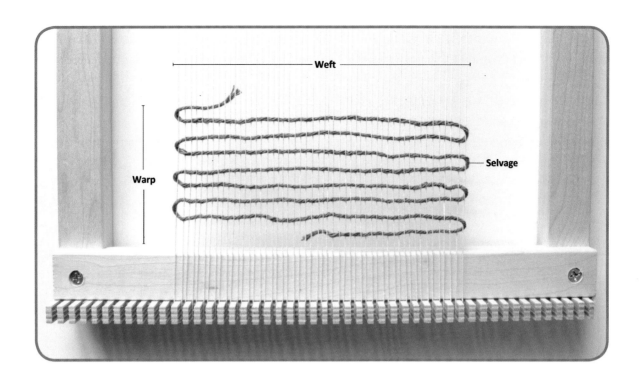

WARP THE LOOM

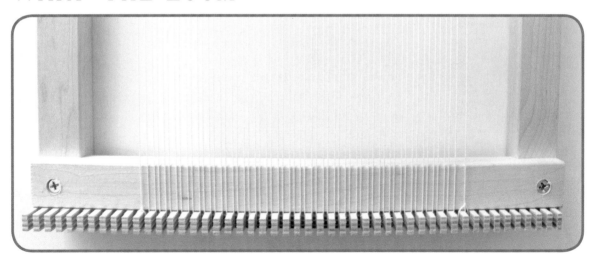

Warping the loom is the first step before starting to weave. The warp is the set of lengthwise yarn or thread that is held in tension on the loom. The yarn that is woven over and under the warp threads is called weft. To warp the loom, follow the steps on the next page.

1. First, decide the width of the piece you're going to make. I decided to center my piece on my loom and counted 10 teeth from each side. This will give me a piece that is 7 inches (18 centimeters) wide. To warp your loom, start at the bottom left of your loom and tie a double knot on the first tooth.

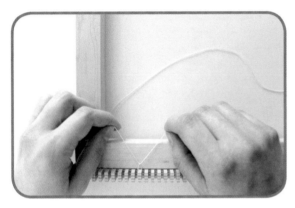

2. Carry the thread up to the top of the loom, turn it over and around the tooth, and bring it down again to the bottom.

3. Pass your warp thread around the next tooth on the bottom of the loom and carry the thread up again. Continue this process until you reach the last tooth of your top warping area.

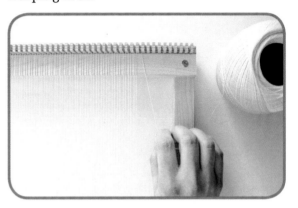

4. To finish, carry the thread again to the bottom. Cut your warp thread with scissors and secure the warp to the loom by tying a double knot again.

NOTE: Always remember to keep some tension on the thread while warping the loom. Check the tension in the end before tying the last double knot. If the tension is right, the warp thread should bounce back when you touch it with a finger, similar to an elastic.

For tips on how to choose the best warp thread, see Chapter 2.

TABBY WEAVE

Tabby weaving, also known as plain weaving, is the process of pulling the weft thread (horizontal thread) over and under the warp thread (vertical thread). This technique creates a simple crisscross pattern that links the vertical and horizontal threads together. This is one of the oldest and most basic techniques you will learn, and it is the foundation of most pieces woven on a loom. A tabby weave is also known for its durability and strength.

1. Begin by threading your tapestry needle with the yarn of your choice. Starting from right to left, begin weaving the weft yarn under the first warp thread and then over the next. Repeat this under-over-under process until you have finished the row.

2. Once you get across to the other side, pull your yarn until the hanging end on the side where you started is about 2 inches (5 centimeters) long. Push your yarn down gently with your beater.

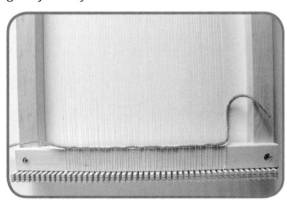

3. In your second row, reverse the alternating sequence of the row below. Work from left to right, passing your weft over and under the warp threads. Make sure you do not pull too tightly on the selvage threads, but also don't let it get too loose.

4. Continue to tabby weave, repeating steps 1 to 3 until you have finished your piece of yarn.

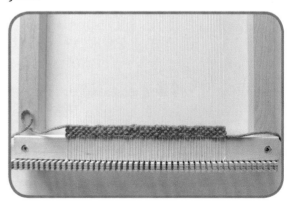

TABBY WEAVE USING A SHED STICK AND A SHUTTLE

The use of a shed stick and a shuttle can be very helpful when tabby weaving large areas using the same yarn. When you are weaving triangles or multiple color areas, it won't be so useful, as you will be changing direction more often.

1. Pass the shed stick through the warp, picking up every other warp thread across the loom the same way you do in tabby weave. The process is the same, but this time you use a shed stick instead of a needle.

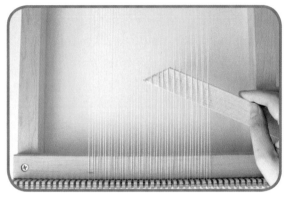

2. Rotate the shed stick to a vertical position, opening a shed (a shed is an open space created between warps that separates your warp threads into upper and lower). Thread your shuttle with a yarn. Pass your shuttle through that shed.

3. Rotate your shed stick back to a horizontal position, closing your shed. Move your shed stick to the top of the loom and push your yarn down with the help of your tapestry beater.

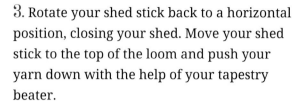

4. Repeat steps 1 through 3 every time you change from 1 row to the other. If you began passing your shed stick *under* the first warp thread on the first row, on the second row you will begin *over* the first warp thread. The use of a shed stick only works in one direction, since the tabby-weave pattern repeats in alternating rows.

When you are weaving, try to be consistent about using the correct amount of tension on the warp for the yarn being used. Also be careful with your weft thread, because it has to have enough slack to be pulled over and under each warp thread. When you don't have the right amount of weft thread, the only option for the warp threads is to move closer together, creating problems in the finished piece. This is called draw-in.

Draw-in is a common problem that many weavers experience, but there are some methods you can use to try to minimize it.

METHODS FOR MINIMIZING DRAW-IN

As you begin weaving, you might notice that the edge of the woven fabric tends to draw in, or tighten. It is caused by pulling the weft thread too tightly across the warp. To keep draw-in to a minimum when you are weaving, instead of having your weft travel straight across the warp, make a curve or an arch with your yarn. Arching and bubbling are clever methods to add length to the weft.

ARCHING

1. Make an arch with your yarn while weaving each row.

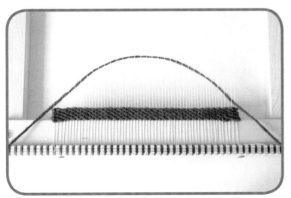

2. Pack it down with your fingers or beater.

BUBBLING

1. Make a curve with your yarn. Using your finger, push down on that curve about every 3 inches (7½ centimeters) so that the curve becomes 3 small bubbles.

2. In the end, pack it down with your fingers or a tapestry beater.

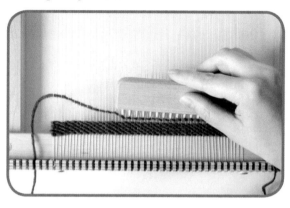

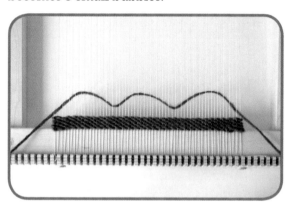

RYA KNOT

Rya is a perfect technique for beginners. It consists of a number of simple and repetitive movements that create little knots of fringe. You won't need any needle or shuttle; all you will need are your hands.

The rya knot is usually used to add texture to your weavings. It can make all the difference in your finished piece. The knots can be long and clipped like on a traditional carpet, or you can play with them and use various lengths and angles.

1. Before starting your rya, I recommend weaving a few rows of tabby weave to work as a support for your knots.

2. Now, start by cutting a few pieces of yarn of the same size (in this example, I cut to 8 inches, or 20¼ centimeters) and lay them on top of your warp threads. Use 3 strands of yarn for each knot.

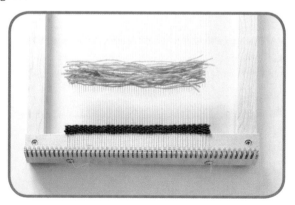

3. Fold the yarn in half and lay it over 2 warp threads. Wrap the left side of the yarn over the outside of the left warp thread, then bring it up from in between the 2 warp threads.

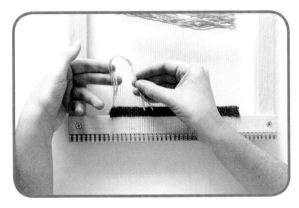

4. Next, wrap the right side of the yarn over the outside of the right warp thread, then bring it up from in between the 2 warp threads.

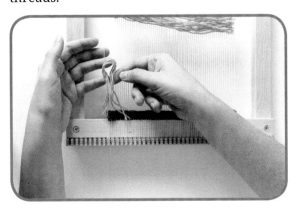

5. Gently lift up the knot to tighten, and bring it down.

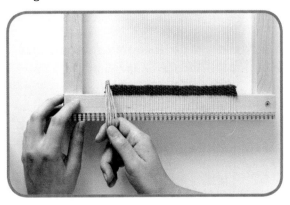

6. Repeat the same process, working with 2 warp threads each time, until you finish your row of rya knots. They will get loose, so make sure you lock them in with at least 2 rows of tabby weave. In the end, trim your knots.

TIME-SAVING TIP FOR MAKING RYA KNOTS

Cutting yarn for your rya knots can be time-consuming, especially if you are thinking of making a lot of knots, so here is a good way to save you some time.

1. Cut a piece of cardboard to approximately the same length that your strands will be. Choose the yarn you will use for the knots.

2. Wrap the yarn around your cardboard as many times as the number of strands you need. Be careful not to tighten your yarn too much around the cardboard, or you will end with less length than you wanted. Use your scissors to cut all the wrapped yarn at the bottom.

3. Now you are ready to make some knots!

DESIGN GEOMETRIC SHAPES

Shapes are often used to create a pattern. There are a number of techniques that you can use to create shapes. These techniques will allow you to create shapes such as a square, rectangular, or triangle. After you learn the basics, you can weave almost any shape you can imagine.

The most common techniques for creating shapes are open slit and weft interlock.

OPEN SLIT TECHNIQUE

Open slit is a method where open slits (open spaces, kind of like button holes) are left in between color changes in the tapestry. This means that instead of having two different yarns that interlock with each other on a common warp, in this technique they are woven in separate blocks. These blocks create a slit (space) on the pattern so it is possible to separate the two parts. Open slit method can be used as straight slit or diagonal slit, which means, as the names suggest, the line between the blocks can be straight or diagonal. This technique is commonly used in kilim rugs, tapestries, and wall art.

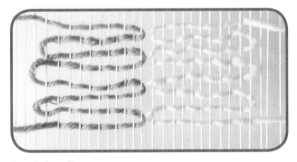

Straight slit

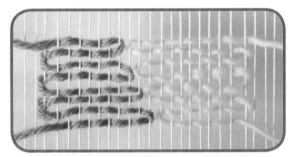

Diagonal slit

WEFT INTERLOCK TECHNIQUE

This technique is used for making blocks of color without leaving open slits in the tapestry fabric. In this technique, two blocks are joined together by interlocking the weft threads, creating a zig-zag look. It's more often used when weaving functional textiles.

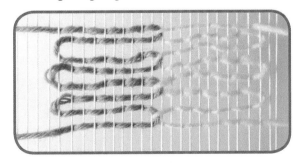

CREATE BLOCKS USING STRAIGHT SLIT

1. Start by doing a tabby weave, from left to right, counting 20 warp strings.

On your 20th string, turn back to your starting point.

2. Continue the process described in step 1 until you finish your first block. Don't forget that in tabby weaving, the yarn passes over and under the warp threads, with the order reversed in alternating rows.

3. Start on the other side of the warp, from right to left, and tabby weave counting your warp threads until you get to the edge of your first block.

4. Weave around the warp thread that is next to the edge of your block and turn back to your starting point. Your yarns have to meet in the center of the 2 blocks but never interlock with each other.

5. Continue to tabby weave until you finish your block.

CREATE TRIANGLES USING DIAGONAL SLIT

1. Get started on your triangle base, weaving your first row using tabby weave. Count 12 warp threads and turn back to your starting point.

2. When you turn around for your next row, you will decrease 1 warp thread on each side of your triangle.

3. Continue creating your triangle, making sure you begin each subsequent row 1 strand closer to the center until you get to the top of the triangle.

4. Your triangle is done.

5. After completing your triangle, you can now begin to fill in the rest of the warp around it using diagonal slit. Start at the edge of the loom and tabby weave until you get to the edge of your triangle. Turn back without interlocking your yarns.

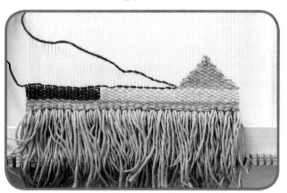

6. Continue in this manner, working your way up the loom. Stop when you have filled all the unwoven space around the triangle.

SOUMAK

Soumak adds texture and dimension to your weave. This technique involves wrapping the weft yarn around the warp threads, resulting in a beautiful raised stitch. It is also known as a braid weave because the final result looks similar to a fishtail braid.

1. Cut 2 long pieces of yarn, each approximately triple the length of your warp width, and tie them together with a knot on one end. The knotted end will be on the left side of your loom and the open end on the right side, with the yarn forming an arch on top of your loom. Start by lifting up the first 2 warp threads. Place the knotted end of your yarn behind those first 2 warps, with the knot coming out on the right of those 2 warps.

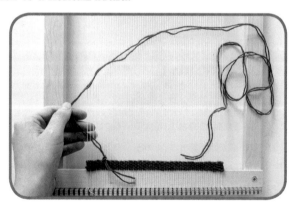

2. Now you will work with the open end of your yarn. Using your left hand, lift up the next 2 warp threads and loop your yarn under and around those warps, going from right to left.

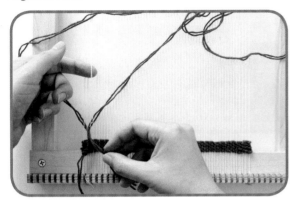

3. Pull the yarn gently down until you touch the base of your weaving. Your first stitch is done.

4. Repeat steps 3 and 4 until you reach the end of your row. Remember that in every step, you need to pass your yarn under and around 2 warp threads, working from right to left. Always lift your yarn up before every stitch.

5. When you reach the end of your first row, you will lift the last 1 or 2 warp threads and pass your yarn underneath. For your next row, you will work from left to right.

6. You are ready to start your second row of soumak. Skip the first 2 warp threads of your second row and lift the next set of 2 warp threads with your right hand.

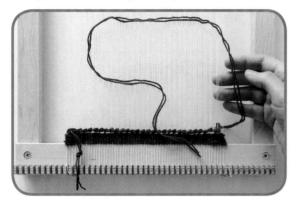

7. Now, using your left hand to hold the weft yarn and while keeping the warp threads in place, use your right hand to pass the yarn under and around those 2 warp threads, moving from left to right.

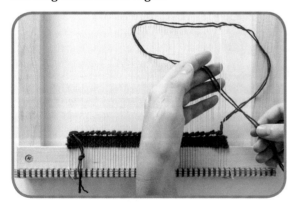

8. Pull the yarn gently down to the base of your weaving.

9. Continue your soumak to the end of the row, repeating steps 7 and 8.

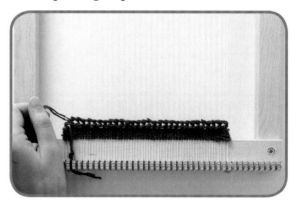

10. Weave the 2 ends in through the back of your tapestry (see instructions for finishing on page 36).

LOOPS

Loops are created by using tabby weave and running the yarn over a round wooden dowel. The yarns are interlaced in such a way that loops are formed on the surface. This is a good option for adding texture to your tapestry.

1. Cut 2 or more pieces of yarn (approximately 2 arm's-lengths) and tie them together with a knot on one end. With the knotted end in your left hand, weave your yarn across the warp threads using tabby weave. When you reach the end of your row, pull your yarn until you have a 2-inch (5-centimeter) tail on your left side.

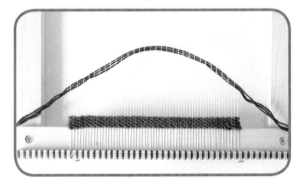

2. Starting on the right side of the loom, pull your yarn up with your finger.

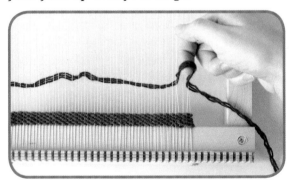

3. Take your wooden needle or dowel stick and put it through the first loop.

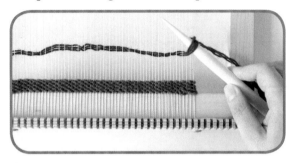

4. Repeat steps 2 and 3 until your dowel is completely wrapped with loops, as shown in the picture below. Push the needle down and bring the loops to the base of your weaving.

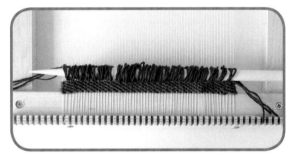

5. Cut another piece of the same yarn and weave 2 or 3 rows of tabby weave above the loops to lock them in.

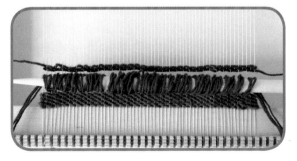

6. Gently remove the dowel so that you leave behind a row of loops. Push the loops down with the help of your beater or comb. Repeat this process for as many rows of loops you want. Remember to lock each row with tabby weave, otherwise the loops will get loose.

7. Your first row of loops is done.

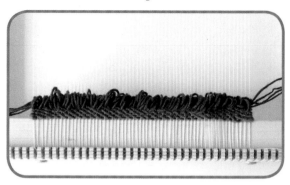

FINISH YOUR WOVEN PIECE

To keep your weft from coming out at the ends of your weaving, you will need to finish it. This is the final step before your project is ready to be hanged or displayed.

There are a number of ways to finish your project, depending on the loom you are using, the type of project you are making, whether it is a decorative or a wearable piece, and even the design or look you prefer for your piece. I have included here my favorite ways to finish a woven piece.

WEAVE IN WEFT AND WARP ENDS

1. First, use your tapestry needle to weave the ends of your weft yarn strands into the back of your piece. Each end should be woven into the corresponding color area. Flip your weave over to make sure that the tails don't show on the front of your woven piece. I recommend doing this step before you take your piece off the loom. The tension of the loom makes it easier to hide those tails.

TIP: I prefer to end my wefts at the beginning or end of my warp. This is just a preference. If you prefer to end your yarn in the middle, just make sure that there's a 4-inch (10-centimeter) tail of yarn left. In the end, tuck that tail through the back of the next available warp thread.

2. On the bottom of your woven piece, cut the warp threads off the loom.

3. Tie the warp threads together, 2 at a time, with double knots.

4. Continue until you have tied all the warp threads together.

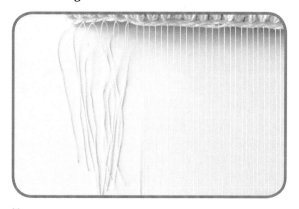

5. With the help of a needle, weave your warp ends in through the back of your tapestry to hide them.

6. If you created a woven piece that will not be hung, like a bracelet or a pillow, weave the top warp ends into the tapestry, following steps 2 through 5. Be sure to leave enough space at the top of your loom so that you can tie the warps more easily.

7. If you've made a wall hanging, take your woven piece off the loom by gently unlooping the top warp threads, 1 at a time. Take your dowel or branch, and loop each strand around it once (or twice, if you have more warp space available). Adjust a few rows of weaving toward the top if you need to.

8. Once your woven piece is off the loom, cut a piece of yarn and tie one end on each side of the dowel. It is now ready to hang.

If you don't want to finish your weave by tying your warp ends, there is an alternative finishing called the hemstitch. Hemstitching is a way to secure your edges in place so that when you take your project off the loom, it does not unravel. It is not a necessary technique to finish your weaving, but is a nice decorative option. It will give your piece a cleaner look in the end, but will take you more time to finish.

HEMSTITCH

1. To finish with hemstitch, first weave 2 or 3 rows using tabby weave. When in the last row, make the last weft comes out on the left side of your loom. Leave a long tail (at least 3 times as long as the warp is wide) and thread it through a tapestry needle. Bring your yarn under and around the last 3 warp threads.

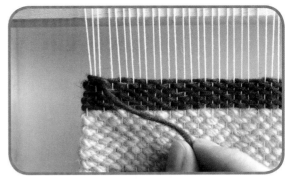

2. Bring the needle out of the back of the woven cloth, 2 rows down. Pull gently to tighten the warps together.

3. Repeat this process for the rest of the warp threads. When you get to the end of the warp, wrap the yarn over the top of the last warp threads and tie off into the back of your weaving. The photo below shows how it will look in the end.

4

PROJECTS

This chapter includes 15 unique and easy-to-follow projects, all fully illustrated with step-by-step photos. You'll learn to make home decor objects, like wall hangings and pillows; wearable items, like a necklace or a bracelet; and beautiful repurposed objects, like a branch or driftwood. These projects cover a variety of loom types: frame loom, circular loom, and even natural objects.

In these projects, you will have the chance to practice all the weaving techniques you have learned in the last chapter, like soumak, tabby weave, and rya knots. They are only examples. The colors, yarns, textures, techniques, sizes, and everything else can be changed and designed your own way.

Now that you have learned the basics, you will be amazed with what you can create!

MAKE YOUR OWN LOOM

When I started my journey through weaving, I didn't wanted to invest in a professional loom to learn the basics. I searched online and realized that I could easily make my own loom at home without spending much. I started with a cardboard loom, using just a piece of reused cardboard, tape, and a cutter. After I learned the basic stitches, I realized I needed a more stable and resistant frame to work that was at the same time portable and easy to use. I made my own frame loom, and now I will teach you how to make yours.

MATERIALS

- 30 x 40-inch (76 x 100-centimeter) wooden canvas frame
- Ruler
- Pencil
- 52 1-inch (2½-centimeter) nails
- Small hammer
- Yarn for warping
- Scissors

DIFFICULTY LEVEL: ⬡ ⬡ ⬡ ⬡ ⬡

INSTRUCTIONS:

1. On the short side of the frame, mark a ½-inch (approximately 1-centimeter) margin toward the inside of the frame with the help of a ruler and a pencil.

2. Then, starting from your initial marking, mark every ½ inch across the top of your frame.

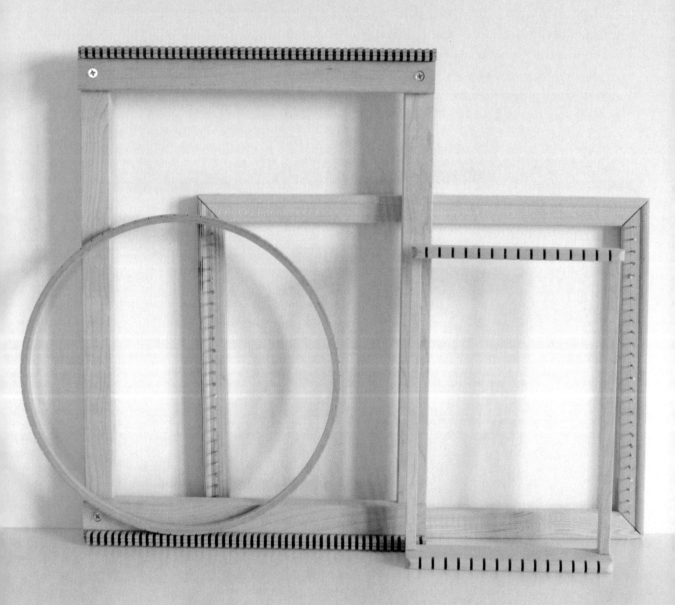

3. Hammer 1 nail into every spot you marked with your pencil.

4. Repeat steps 1 to 3 on the bottom of your frame.

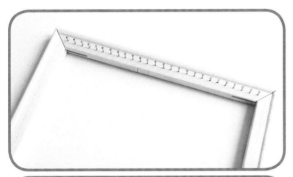

5. Grab the yarn and start warping your homemade loom. Start at the bottom left of your loom and tie a double knot on the first nail. Carry the thread up to the top of the loom, over and around the first nail, and back down again to the next nail on the bottom of the loom. Continue this process until you reach the last nail on the bottom of your loom. Use the scissors to cut the yarn. Tie a double knot in the end.

You have just made a frame loom in about half an hour and without spending almost anything!

MY FIRST WOVEN WALL HANGING

A few years ago when I started weaving, this was one of the first woven projects I made and was really proud of. I think it's a perfect project to learn and practice your weaving skills, since it requires almost every technique I teach in this book. In this project, you will use cotton and wool yarn, and create different textures and geometric designs.

MATERIALS

- 12 x 16-inch (30½ x 40½-centimeter) weaving loom
- Cotton warp yarn
- Cardboard spacer
- Worsted weight wool rug yarn in white, coral, light blue, and peach
- Lace weight single-ply wool yarn in beige
- Worsted weight wool yarn in light peach
- Worsted weight cotton yarn in teal
- Weaving shuttle
- Tapestry needle
- Beater
- Scissors
- Approximately 10-inch (25-centimeter) wooden dowel

FINISHED SIZE: 8 x 16 inches (20 x 42 centimeters) including fringe

DIFFICULTY LEVEL:

INSTRUCTIONS:

1. Warp your loom starting with a double knot on the 10th tooth from the bottom left. Wrap your warp thread up and down the loom until you end up with an 8½-inch (21-centimeter) warping area. Tie a double knot in the end. Check the tension on the warp.

2. Weave a piece of cardboard along your warp (start on one side of the loom and use the same under-over-under technique until you reach the other side of your loom).

Above your cardboard, starting from right to left, weave 3 rows of tabby weave using the white yarn. This will support the fringe, which you will add next.

BEGINNER TIP: With smaller wall hangings, I usually use a spacer, such as a piece of cardboard, a shed stick, or ruler, to allow me to start on the middle of my loom and keep my weaving in place while working. This prevents the piece from ending up with one side smaller than the other and also helps when you are tying off your finished piece.

3. To create a fringe, you will add an entire row of rya knots above your first rows of tabby weave. Using the scissors, cut 62 16-inch (40-centimeter) pieces of white wool yarn. Fold them in half and use 2 pieces of yarn for each knot. (See instructions for rya knots on page 26.)

4. Weave 5 rows of tabby weave, using the same color yarn, on top of your rya knots to secure them. Use the beater to push the weft yarn into place.

5. Grab the coral wool yarn and cut 2 pieces to 32 inches (80 centimeters) long. Start on the left side of your loom and weave 1 row of soumak weaving. Weave each knot over 2 warp threads. When you get to the end of your first row, turn back and continue your soumak until you have created a beautiful soumak braid (see instructions for soumak on page 32).

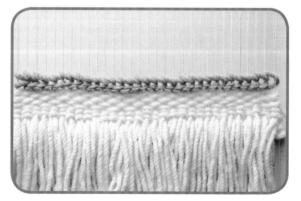

6. Change to your beige yarn and cut a 1-yard length. Weave 3 blocks, with 5 rows each, in tabby weave. You might have to add more yarn to complete all 3 blocks.

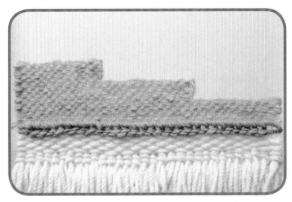

7. Cut 3 pieces of light blue, light peach, and teal yarn to the same length (approximately 16 inches, or 40 centimeters). Use the light peach yarn to weave 1 block, filling the unwoven space on the right side of the loom. When you weave separate blocks together, the 2 different yarns should meet in the middle but not interlock with each other (see instructions for open slit on page 29).

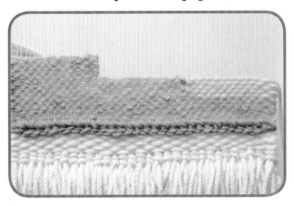

8. After you have finished your f͏   ͏,
repeat the instructions for bloc͏   ͏ ͏ and 3 in light blue and teal. For the light blue block, start in the middle of your loom. Count 17

warp threads to the right, then turn back to your starting point. Weave 5 rows of tabby weave to finish the block. For the teal block, fill the empty unwoven space on the right side of your loom. In the remaining space on the left, weave 8 rows using the teal yarn.

9. Weave 14 rows of tabby weave with white yarn. Every time you run out of yarn in the middle of your process, leave a 3-inch tail end and start another piece of yarn. You will weave in all the tails in the end.

10. Cut 2 pieces of white yarn to 32 inches (80 centimeters) and weave 2 rows using soumak. On top of that, add 5 rows of tabby weave, still using the white yarn.

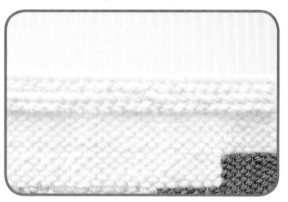

11. Continue with the white yarn. On the left side of your loom, start weaving a block using 16 warp threads.

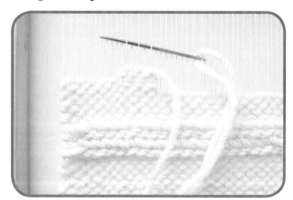

12. Cut 10 pieces of the teal yarn to 6 inches (15 centimeters). Add 5 rya knots, using 2 pieces of yarn for each knot, in the middle of your block. Finish the block with 4 more rows of the white yarn.

13. Change to the beige yarn and weave a block with 8 rows of tabby weave on the right side of your loom, filling the unwoven space left. Add 4 more rows of tabby weave on top of that.

14. To finish this project, you need to master one last challenge: the triangle shape. This might look difficult, but once you have made your first one, you will see it's rather simple. You are going to weave 3 triangles in 3 different colors: coral, peach, and light blue. First, cut 3 pieces of yarn to approximately 1 yard, one of each color. Take 1 of those pieces and start weaving on the right side of your loom. Weave over and under, counting 20 warps. On the 20th warp, turn back to your starting point. Continue with that method, decreasing the number of warps after each row until you get to the top of the triangle (see instructions for diagonal slit on page 31).

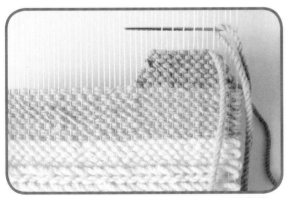

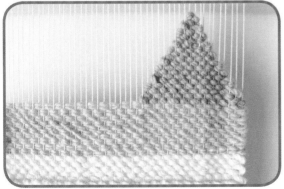

15. Repeat the same process for the other 2 triangles. Start the middle triangle on your 22nd warp. Count 20 warps and turn back, using the same process described in step 14. Your final triangle will start on the 43rd warp thread. Each triangle is made with 20 warps.

16. Fill all the unwoven space around the triangles with white yarn. Add a few rows of tabby weave until you reach the top of your loom.

FINISHING STEPS:

17. Weave all your ends into the back of your tapestry.

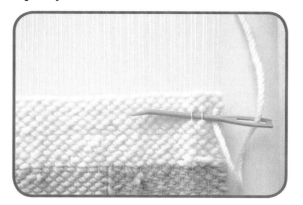

18. Take it off the loom by cutting the bottom warps as close to the loom as you can, and then tie them in pairs with double knots. With the help of a needle, hide them on the back of your tapestry. Unloop the top warp threads and leave them uncut. Insert your dowel through the loops, gently adjusting a few rows of weaving towards the top. Cut a length of your cotton warp yarn and tie knots on each end of your dowel. (See instructions for finishing your weaving on page 36.)

19. Hang it on a wall, and be proud of what you have created!

WOVEN NECKLACE

This fiber art necklace is easy to make and the perfect statement piece to add to your closet. It is another chance for you to practice your weaving skills and create a one-of-a-kind handmade piece that you can use proudly wherever you go.

MATERIALS

- Weaving loom at least 20 inches (50 centimeters) high
- Thick cotton warp thread
- Worsted weight cotton yarn in white and copper colors
- Tapestry needle
- Scissors

FINISHED SIZE: 1½ x 11 inches (4 x 28 centimeters)

DIFFICULTY LEVEL:

INSTRUCTIONS:

1. Start with a double knot on the bottom left side of your loom and wrap your yarn up and down the loom until you have a 2-inch-wide (5-centimeter-side) warp. Cut the thread and make another double knot. Be sure to have an even number of warp threads. With the white yarn, weave 3 rows of tabby weave. (See instructions for tabby weave on page 23.)

2. Using the scissors, cut 27 strands of white yarn to approximately 7 inches (17¾ centimeters) and create a fringe with rya knots, using 3 strands of yarn for each rya knot. Make 1 rya knot for every 2 warp threads (see instructions for rya knots on page 26).

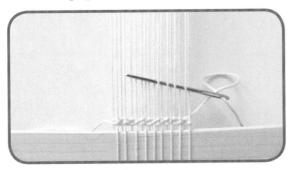

3. Create a diagonal shape above your rya fringe using tabby weave. Cut 1 arm's-length of yarn and start weaving from left to right. Decrease 2 warp threads in each new row you make.

4. Using the copper-colored yarn, add a diagonal row of rya knots on top of the shape you just created. Use the same length and number of strands from step 2.

5. Secure the rya knots with a few rows of tabby weave using the white yarn. Continue weaving in a diagonal shape, filling the unwoven space on the right side. Add a couple of rows using the copper yarn to create a contrast. When finished, you should now have a woven piece that is approximately 1½ inches (4 centimeters) wide.

6. In this step, you will split your single woven piece into 2 separate blocks of the same size. Using the white yarn, start weaving from right to left and count 9 warp threads. On the 9th warp, turn back to your starting point. Begin your second row and continue doing the same thing while you weave up on the loom. Add a couple rows using the copper yarn, then switch back to the white yarn. Repeat the same process with your left side block. When the 2 yarns meet in the middle, they should not interlock with each other (see instructions for open slit on page 29).

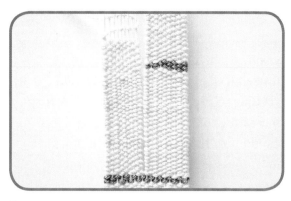

7. On your left side, add a few rows of the copper yarn to finish the top left of your necklace.

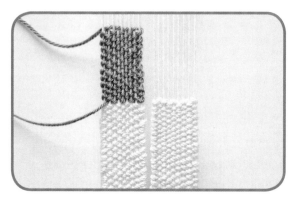

8. Finish the right block with white yarn. Stop when you have 2 blocks that are 6 inches (15 centimeters) high. The result is a minimal and neutral necklace that you can use with almost every piece in your closet. If you prefer a bright and colorful piece, choose a different color scheme and create your own, one-of-a-kind piece using the instructions you have learned in this tutorial.

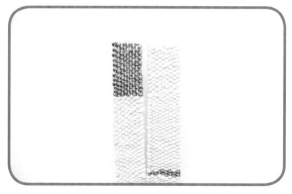

9. Take it off the loom, cutting your top and bottom warps as long as you can. On the bottom, tie your warps together in groups of 2 or 3.

10. Use the top warps to tie your necklace around your neck. Wear it as many times as you like.

BRANCH WEAVING

I like to spend time surrounded by nature and collect special finds during my walks. I often come home with natural branches, wildflowers, and shells. In one of those walks, I found this beautiful branch and thought it was perfect for a weaving project.

For this piece, I used a variety of yarns, such as wool, cotton, and merino roving, but you can use fabric leftovers, beads, and whatever else you have around. This is supposed to be a fun project; don't stick too much to the instructions, and experiment with different yarns and techniques. Follow your imagination—you can't go wrong!

This project will allow you to bring some nature to your home as a unique art piece.

MATERIALS

+ One stick or branch with a V shape
+ A thick and resistant 100% cotton warp yarn
+ Wool and cotton yarns with different colors and thicknesses for weaving (Suggestion: try mixing light worsted weight yarns with bulky weight yarns)
+ Scissors
+ Tapestry needle
+ Beater

FINISHED SIZE: 40 x 12 inches (102 x 31 centimeters)

DIFFICULTY LEVEL:

INSTRUCTIONS:

1. In this project, the branch works as a natural loom. To warp your loom, start by tying your cotton yarn in a double knot at the bottom of your "V" area, leaving a 2-inch (5-centimeter) tail.

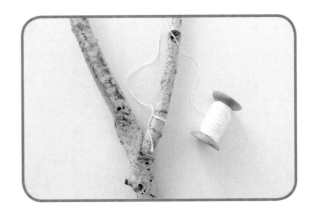

2. Loop your yarn around each branch twice and make sure it is quite tight. Try to leave the same space between strands of warp.

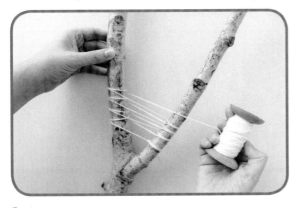

3. When you get to the end of your desired warping area, tie a double knot. The warp should be pretty tight but not too tight, or it will add too much pressure to the sticks. The final result should look like this.

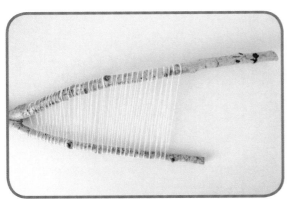

4. Now that you have your warp ready, it's time to weave. Using approximately 1 yard of a lighter color yarn of thin texture, start at the bottom right and use your tapestry needle to weave over and under the warp string in a tabby weave. When you get to the end of each row, push the yarn down gently with your beater.

5. Continue weaving until you run out of yarn. Remember that the second row will have the opposite pattern of the one you began with. In tabby weave, the pattern repeats on alternate rows (see instructions for tabby weave on page 23).

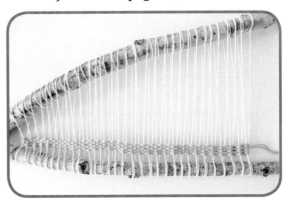

6. Choose a thicker yarn to weave (I used a bulky yarn) and cut 1 yard length. Repeat the same process as before, using tabby weave.

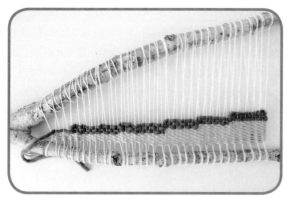

7. Continue experimenting with different yarns, colors, and thicknesses until you reach the top of your warp. I used bright colors and different textured yarns, like thick wool roving, to create a beautiful bubbling effect.

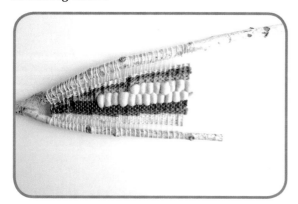

8. To finish your woven branch, thread your needle with the tail ends and weave into the back of your tapestry using the basic over and under stitch.

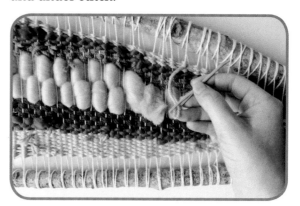

DESERT VIBES WALL HANGING

This wall hanging's simple design plays with coordinating neutrals and earthy tones to create a visually appealing piece. Use only three or four colors and explore all their different shades. Choose textured yarns, create the impression of movement by adding multiple layers of fringe, and create an interesting design by adding geometric shapes. Let's do this!

MATERIALS

- Weaving loom
- Cotton warp yarn
- Cardboard spacer
- Scissors
- Tapestry needle
- Lace weight single-ply wool yarn in peach, terracotta, light gray, and beige
- Bulky weight wool yarn in gray
- Worsted weight wool yarn in cream
- Beater
- Shed stick
- Shuttle
- Approximately 9-inch (23-centimeter) wooden dowel

FINISHED SIZE: 7 x 17 inches (18 x 43 centimeters) including fringe

DIFFICULTY LEVEL:

INSTRUCTIONS:

1. Warp your frame loom following the warping instructions on page 21. You will need to have an 8-inch-wide (21-centimeter-wide) warp. Check the tension on the warp. Use a piece of cardboard to keep your woven piece in place since you will start to weave on the middle of the loom.

2. Cut 1 yard of peach yarn and thread your tapestry needle with the yarn. Start on the right side of your loom using tabby weave, and complete 2 rows. On the third row, you will stop on your 44th warp thread and turn back, creating a block. Weave 3 blocks, with 9 rows each, in tabby weave. You might have to add more yarn several times to complete all 3 blocks, each spanning 15 warp threads. Leave at least 4 inches (10 centimeters) of tail every time you change yarn.

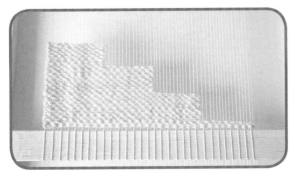

3. Add a layer of rya knots on top of the first block of tabby weave on the right side of your loom. Cut 24 strands of the same peach yarn and use 3 at a time to make your knots. When you choose a thin yarn for your rya knots, you might have to increase the number of strands you use for each knot in order to achieve the desired effect. (See instructions for rya knots on page 26.)

4. On top of those rya knots, weave a new block with 7 rows using the terracotta yarn. Use the open slit technique (page 29) to weave the peach and the terracotta blocks together. This means the 2 different yarns should meet in the middle but not interlock with each other, leaving a slit between them.

5. Keep repeating steps 3 and 4 for each of the other terracotta blocks. Create 4 blocks with the same size and color. Make sure you do not pull your selvage edges too tightly at the end of each row; keep the tension even on each side of your piece.

6. Thread your needle with the gray yarn. Create another block right above your terracotta block using tabby weave. Again, use the open slit technique. Don't interlock your yarns or you will loose the desired effect.

7. Fill all the unwoven space until you reach the top of your last terracotta block. Use your beater to help you push the yarn down after each row and keep a tight weave. Add 6 more rows of tabby weave. Then, cut 2 strands of your gray yarn approximately 2 arm's-lengths. Weave 2 rows using the soumak technique (see instructions for soumak on page 32).

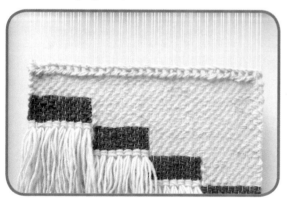

8. Use your shed stick and a shuttle to weave 5 rows of tabby weave using the gray bulky yarn. The shed stick will only help you finish your weaving faster.

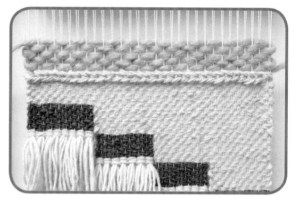

9. Change to your cream yarn and weave 6 rows using tabby weave.

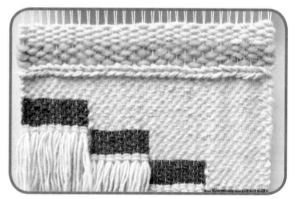

10. Continue using the simplest form of weaving, the tabby weave technique. With a thinner beige yarn, weave 12 rows. Notice that you're constantly changing yarn. This will give you a more textured and visually pleasing woven piece in the end. Always try to use different textures and colors while you are weaving, but be careful that all the colors look good next to each other.

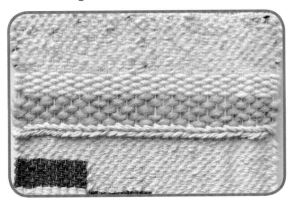

11. Grab your terracotta yarn again and weave 3 rows of tabby weave. Since you are approaching the top of your loom, finish your piece using the soumak technique. (I often end my pieces with a soumak braid. I think soumak gives a more clean finish to tapestry once you take it off the loom.)

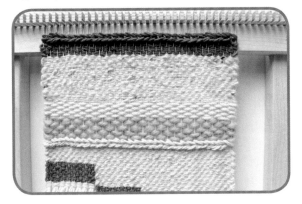

12. Looking at the finished tapestry, I realized I needed to add more texture in the fringe at the bottom. Sometimes that happens, and that's fine. Go to the bottom of your piece and add another row of rya knots below the existing peach fringe using the gray bulky yarn. This will add movement and texture. Cut 60 strands to approximately 15 inches (38 centimeters) each. Use 2 strands of yarn for each knot. This row of rya knots will be your bottom and final fringe.

FINISHING STEPS:

13. Clean the back side of your piece, weaving in all the tail ends. Use a tapestry needle and stitch each yarn in the corresponding color area so that it doesn't show on the front of your piece. Trim the excess. I recommend doing this step before you take your piece off the loom because it makes your job easier.

14. Cut your bottom warps and tie them together in pairs. Be careful not to pull your knots too tight, or you could affect the shape of your piece. Hide them on the back.

15. Unloop the top warp threads and leave them uncut.

16. Insert your dowel through the loops, gently adjusting a few rows of weaving toward the top.

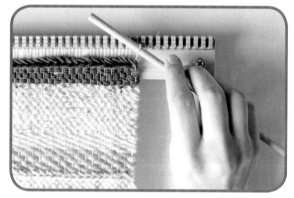

17. Cut a length of your cotton warp yarn and tie knots on each end of your dowel. It is ready to hang on a wall.

EVERYDAY COASTER

This project is pretty simple and quick to make. I remember when I was in school, I made a woven coaster using fabric leftovers in art classes. I was 12 years old. I'm sure everyone can make this project and I think it is a fun project to make with your kids.

MATERIALS

- Weaving loom
- Cotton warp yarn
- Cardboard spacer
- Cotton yarn in white, aqua blue, and multicolored
- Tapestry needle
- Beater or weaving comb
- Scissors

FINISHED PIECE: 4 x 4 inches (10 x 10 centimeters)

DIFFICULTY LEVEL: ⬡ ⬡ ⬡ ⬡ ⬡

INSTRUCTIONS:

1. Warp your loom with a thick cotton yarn. The warping width will be approximately 4½ inches wide. Start weaving about 1 inch (approximately 2 centimeters) from the bottom of the loom. Use a piece of cardboard if you need to help keep your weaving in place while working.

2. Start your first row by passing the multicolored yarn under and over in a tabby weave. Finish your first row and leave a 3-inch (7½-centimeter) tail on it. On the second row, work in an opposite pattern from the first row. If you went under the last warp thread on the first row, you must now start by going over the first warp thread on the second row.

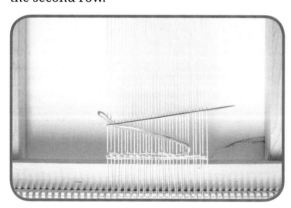

3. Change to your white yarn and continue this alternate pattern until you have completed 7 rows of tabby weave. Don't pull your yarn too much on the end of the rows, or you will affect the structure of your piece. After each row, push your yarn down with the help of your beater or weaving comb.

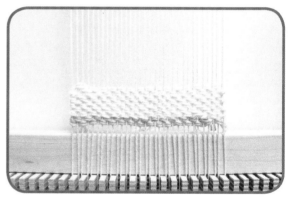

4. Next, use the aqua blue yarn and weave 3 rows using the same technique as before. End your yarn in the beginning of the 4th row.

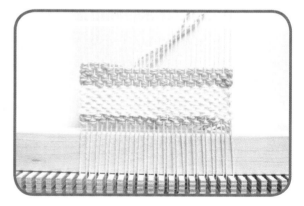

5. Use the multicolored yarn again, and start where you ended the last thread. Weave 14 rows using that same yarn.

6. Change to the aqua blue yarn and do 3 rows of tabby weave followed by 7 rows of the white yarn. Finish with 2 rows of the multicolored yarn. You should end up with a symmetrical pattern.

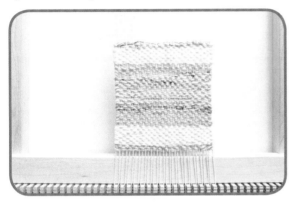

7. Once you finished your coaster, take it off the loom, cutting your warps on the top and bottom of your loom. Leave the ends long.

8. Join the strings in pairs of 2, making a double knot on each end. In this project, you don't have to weave in the warp ends on the back of your tapestry; the ends will work as a fringe and become part of the final piece.

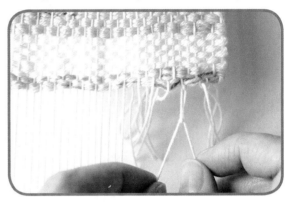

9. You have made a beautiful coaster to use every day when you drink your coffee or tea.

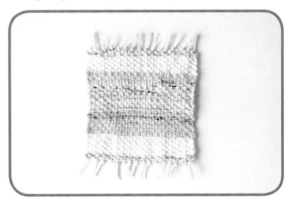

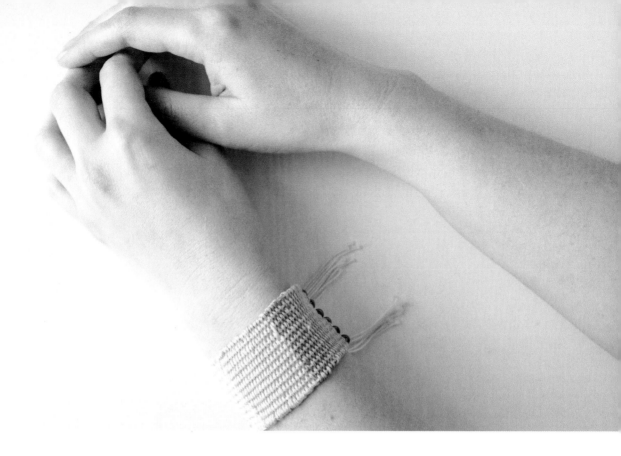

SUMMER BRACELET

The fun thing about weaving is that once you have learned the basic stitches and techniques, you can get out of your comfort zone and try to do different things with your loom. This woven bracelet is an easy and quick project that you can do in a couple of hours. It is perfect to wear on summer days.

MATERIALS

- Weaving loom
- Thick cotton warp yarn
- Tapestry needle
- Light worsted weight cotton yarn in white, tan, light pink, and pastel pink
- Off-white silk yarn
- Brass beads (or other embellishment of your choice)
- Scissors

FINISHED SIZE: 1½ x 4½ inches (4 x 12 centimeters)

DIFFICULTY LEVEL: ⬡⬡⬡⬡⬡

INSTRUCTIONS:

1. Start with a double knot at the 18th tooth and wrap your yarn up and down the loom until you have a 1½-inch (4-centimeter) warping area. Tie a double knot on the end. Grab your white cotton yarn, thread a needle, and start weaving 5½ inches (14 centimeters) from the bottom of your loom (this is important because you will need to have long warp ends to wrap the bracelet around your wrist). Count 12 rows of tabby weave. Change to the tan yarn and weave 3 more rows (see instructions for tabby weave on page 23).

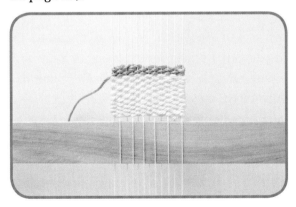

2. Next, use the off-white silk yarn to weave another 10 rows of tabby weave. Make sure you don't pull too tightly on the selvage edges at the end of each row, or you will affect the shape of your bracelet. Use your beater, or your fingers, to help push the yarn down after each row and keep a tight weave (see instructions to minimize draw-in on page 25).

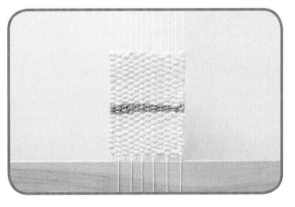

3. Use your light pink cotton yarn to weave approximately 30 rows using tabby weave.

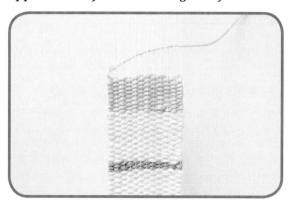

Then, add 10 more rows of the tan yarn. When you need to change your yarn color, make sure to leave at least 3-inch (7½-centimeter) long tails; you will weave them into the back of your piece in the end.

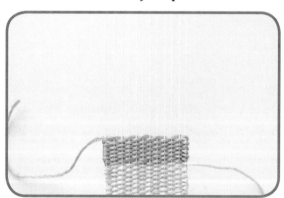

4. To finish your piece, use the pastel pink yarn. Stop when you have woven about 4½ inches (12 centimeters) up the loom, or when you think your bracelet is big enough.

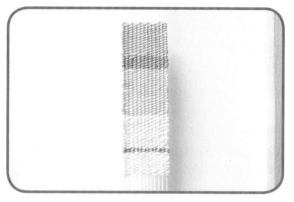

5. Weave all the tails of yarn into the back of your piece. Use the scissors to carefully cut the bottom warp threads and tie them together in pairs. Do the same to your top warps. Cut the warps as close to the loom as you can. Remember you need to have enough length to wrap the bracelet around your wrist.

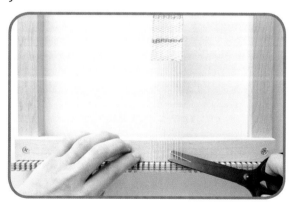

6. Choose 2 warps at a time and add a brass bead, or any other embellishment you prefer, and tie your warps together in 1 knot (the knot should secure your bead in place). Do the same on the other end of your bracelet. (You can also braid all your warps together to add a special final effect.)

7. Use your one-of-a-kind bracelet all the time!

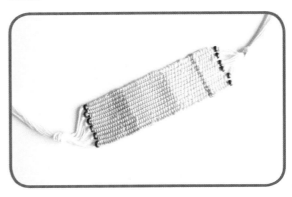

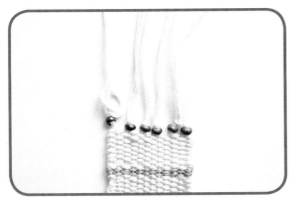

FLUFFY WALL HANGING

In this project you can experiment weaving with plenty of different colors and textures. I must confess I'm always drawn to pastels and neutral colors and my projects end up being similar in color, but sometimes it is good to change and experiment with other color schemes. In this project, you will weave with thick yarns, like a bulky yarn, and learn to weave using wool roving. You will get the chance to practice your looping skills and add plenty of rya knots to create a beautiful fringed woven piece. I think this colorful tapestry would look lovely in a kid's room!

MATERIALS

- Weaving loom
- Cotton warp thread
- Cardboard spacer
- Tapestry needle
- Worsted weight wool yarn in white, gray, and yellow
- Worsted weight cotton yarn in light blue and teal
- Light weight wool yarn in gray
- Bulky weight wool yarn in teal,
- Super bulky roving in pink
- Shed stick
- Shuttle
- Beater
- Scissors
- Dowel or big needle
- Approximately 11-inch (28-centimeter) wooden dowel

FINISHED SIZE: 10 x 20 inches (25 x 50 centimeters) including fringe

DIFFICULTY LEVEL: ⬡⬡⬡⬡⬡

INSTRUCTIONS:

1. Warp your frame loom with the cotton warp thread. You will need to have an 10½-inch-wide (27-centimeter-wide) warping. Check the tension on the warp after each turn on the loom; you don't want a loose or too-tight warp. Use a piece of cardboard and weave it in across the warp. Weave 3 rows of tabby weave with the help of a shed stick and a shuttle; this will support your fringe (see shuttle instructions on page 24).

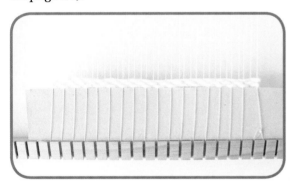

2. Move your shed stick to the top of your loom. You won't need it for this next step. Using the scissors, cut 36 strands of the gray wool yarn to 20 inches (50 centimeters) each. Make a row of rya knots using 2 warp threads for each knot. The number of total yarn strands you will use will depend on the thickness of the yarn. The thinner the yarn, the more strands of yarn you will need to create the desired textured effect.

3. Move your shed stick to the bottom of your loom and, with the help of your shuttle, weave 15 rows using the tabby weave technique. Use the tapestry beater to push your yarn down after each row. Make sure you keep your tension even on both sides of your selvages after each row. Don't pull too tightly, but also don't leave it too loose.

4. Now, make a row of rya knots using the light blue and teal threads. First, cut 30 strands of the light blue cotton yarn to 18 inches (46 centimeters) long each. On the right side of your loom, make 5 rya knots using 3 strands of yarn for each.

5. Repeat step 4 on the left side of your loom. In the middle of the loom, use your teal wool yarn to make 8 rya knots. For these last knots, you will need 24 strands of yarn that are 24 inches (60 centimeters) each. Again, use 3 strands of yarn for each knot.

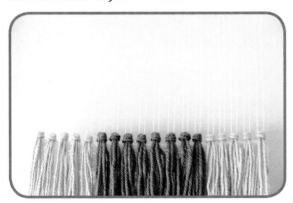

6. On top of those rya knots, make another row of rya using the white wool yarn. Cut 54 strands of yarn to 6 inches (15 centimeters) and make 18 rya knots with 3 strands of yarn each.

7. Push your shed stick down again and weave 8 rows of tabby weave in white.

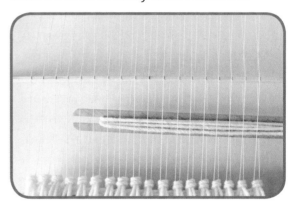

8. Change to the yellow wool yarn and weave 4 rows using tabby weave. On top of that, make another row using the soumak technique (see instructions for soumak on page 32). For the soumak, cut 2 pieces of yellow yarn to approximately 2 yards.

9. Change back to the gray wool yarn. Weave 10 rows using tabby weave. Then, cut 3 pieces of the light weight gray yarn to approximately 50 inches (130 centimeters) and knot them together on one end. Start by weaving your yarn over and under until you reach the end of your row, then with the help of a dowel or a big needle, start making a row of loops. (See instructions for loops on page 35.)

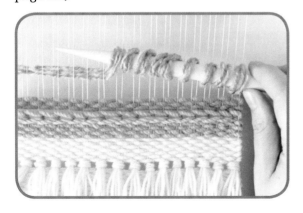

10. Finish your first row of loops and lock the loops with 2 rows of tabby weave using the same gray yarn. Make another row of loops, repeating all the steps you made for the first row. Again, lock them in with 2 rows of tabby weave before you remove your dowel stick.

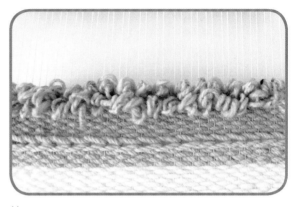

11. Use the light blue yarn again to weave 8 rows using tabby weave.

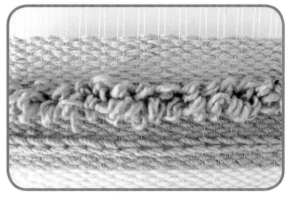

12. Grab the teal bulky wool yarn and cut 2 yards. Weave 1 row of soumak. Add 3 rows of tabby weave using the same yarn.

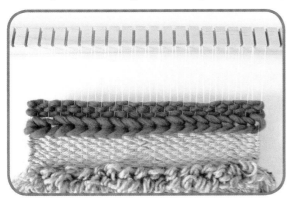

13. Using wool roving is another way to add texture to your piece. Cut a piece of the pink roving to half a yard and weave, passing the yarn under and over the warp threads, as you would with a tabby weave, except this time, you need to weave under the first warp thread and over the next 2 warps. Continue

that pattern until you reach the end of the row. In the places where you weaved over 2 warp threads, push the yarn up just a bit to create that cute "bubble" effect.

14. Since you are approaching the top of your loom, end your piece with 6 rows of tabby weave using the gray wool yarn. Finish with 2 rows of soumak using the same yarn.

FINISHING STEPS:

15. Clean the back side of your piece, weaving in all the tail ends. Use a tapestry needle and stitch each yarn in the corresponding color area so it doesn't show on the front of your piece. Trim the excess. Cut your bottom warps and tie them together in pairs. Be careful not to pull your knots too tight. Hide them on the back with the help of a needle (see finishing instructions on page 36).

16. Unloop the top warp threads and leave them uncut. Insert your dowel through the loops. Cut a length of your cotton warp yarn and tie knots on each end of your dowel. Trim all your rya-knot fringes using right and diagonal angles, creating a geometric layered effect.

17. Hang it in your kids' room. They will love it.

TINY FRAMED WEAVING

This project is the perfect size to be done on a summer afternoon. Take a smaller loom outside and sit in your garden or any other place you like. When you finish, put it in a small frame (why not?) and add a bit of texture to your bedside table.

MATERIALS

- Weaving loom
- 10 x 10-inch (25 x 25-centimeter) photo frame
- Black cotton warp yarn
- Dark gray, chunky yellow, and light gray wool yarn
- Tapestry needle
- Scissors
- Dowel or large wooden needle
- Tapestry beater or comb

FINISHED SIZE: 5 x 6½ inches (12 x 16 centimeters) including fringe

DIFFICULTY LEVEL:

INSTRUCTIONS:

1. Start by tying a double knot on the top of your loom. Wrap your black warp thread up and down the loom until your warping space is about 5½ inches (14 centimeters) wide. Tie a double knot in the end. (Be careful not to exceed your frame space.) Using the tapestry needle, start weaving 3 inches (7½ centimeters) above the bottom of your loom. Weave 3 rows of tabby weave using the dark gray yarn. On top of that, weave a row of rya knots. Use the scissors to cut 84 pieces of the same yarn to 4 inches (10 centimeters). Make 21 rya knots, using 4 pieces of yarn for each knot (see instructions for rya knots on page 26).

2. Grab the yellow chunky yarn and cut 42 strands to the same size (approximately 3 inches or 7 centimeters). Use 2 pieces of yarn for each knot. Weave these rya knots immediately above the gray knots. (You might notice that when I make rya knots, I sometimes use more than 2 pieces of yarn for 1 knot; that number depends on the thickness of the yarn I'm using. When I use a thicker yarn, fewer strands are needed to create a fluffy effect.)

3. Weave 3 rows of tabby weave to secure your knots. Use the dark gray yarn.

4. Add 10 rows of tabby weave using the light gray yarn. Check the tension on your warp edges after each row. In the end, pack your yarn down with the help of your tapestry beater or comb.

5. Create a row of loops, using 3 pieces of light gray yarn, each measuring 2 arm's-lengths. Make a knot on 1 end of the yarn and weave over and under the warp threads until you get to the end of the row. Then, with the help of a large wooden needle or a dowel, slowly create your loops (see instructions for loops on page 35).

6. Finish your loops and weave 3 rows of tabby weave, using the chunky yellow yarn, to help secure your loops in place.

7. Finally, weave 5 rows of tabby weave with the dark gray yarn.

8. To take it off the loom, cut the warp ends on the top and bottom of your loom.

9. Tie the warp threads together in pairs. Hide them on the back of your tapestry.

10. Use a double-sided tape and stick your tapestry to a white piece of cardboard (it really has to be a thick and resistant paper). Frame it for a wall or your bedside table.

WOVEN KEYCHAIN

This simple, easy-to-make project is very useful—you can use it every day. Who doesn't need a cute keychain?

MATERIALS

- Weaving loom
- Thick cotton warp thread
- Wool yarn in dark blue, bright pink, peach, and light gray
- Cotton/wool yarn in mint
- Tapestry needle
- Cardboard spacer
- Scissors
- Key ring

FINISHED SIZE: 1½ x 4½ inches (4 centimeters x 12 centimeters)

DIFFICULTY LEVEL:

INSTRUCTIONS:

1. Warp your loom with a thick cotton yarn. Start with a double knot on the top of the loom and wrap your yarn up and down the loom, ending with another double knot. Your warp space should be around 1½ inches (3¾ centimeters) wide.

2. Cut a strand of dark blue yarn approximately 20 inches long. Start weaving in the middle of your loom (use a piece of cardboard to keep your weaving in place, if needed). Weave 18 rows, or approximately 1 inch (2½ centimeters) of tabby weave (see instructions for tabby weave on page 23).

3. Change to the mint yarn and continue using tabby weave for 12 rows. Now change to the bright pink yarn and continue using tabby weave for 3 rows. Make sure you don't pull too tightly on the selvage edges at the end of each row, keeping an even tension. Every time you change yarns, make sure you leave at a tail that is at least 3 inches (7½ centimeters) long; you will weave them in into the back of your piece in the end.

3. Choose another bright color, like peach, to create contrast and interest. I used colors like mint, bright pink, and peach because I wanted this project to be colorful and fun. Finish with the light gray yarn. Stop when you have woven about 3½ inches (9 centimeters) up in the loom. Check the tension on the selvages after each row.

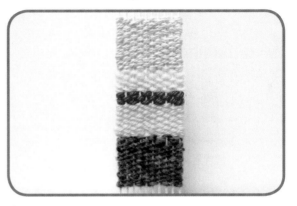

4. Weave all the tails of yarn into the back of your piece. Carefully cut the bottom warp threads and tie them together in pairs. Don't cut the warps too short; leave them long because this will be your fringe.

5. Cut your top warps and secure them to the key ring by tying double knots on the back.

BOHO PILLOW

Once you have improved your weaving skills and start feeling comfortable experimenting with new things, you can start making all kinds of woven pieces for your home. This project could seem a bit overwhelming at first because it's a big project, but it's really not that difficult. It just takes more time and patience. In this piece, you will experiment and practice another form of weaving, called freeform weaving. This will create pattern and movement by weaving abstract forms, resulting in a more organic design. I promise you will love the end result!

MATERIALS

- Weaving loom at least 20 inches (50 centimeters) wide
- Thick cotton warp yarn
- Scissors
- Tapestry needle
- Worsted weight wool rug yarn in white and black
- Worsted weight cotton yarn in light blue
- Bulky weight wool yarn in teal and gray
- Lace weight wool yarn in yellow
- Shed stick
- Shuttle
- Beater
- White fabric
- Pillow stuffing
- Measuring tape
- Head pins
- Sewing machine

FINISHED SIZE: 16 x 12 inches (40 x 30 centimeters)

DIFFICULTY LEVEL: ✹ ✹ ✹ ✹ ✹

INSTRUCTIONS:

1. Warp your loom starting with a double knot on the top left and wrap your yarn up and down the loom. End with another double knot on the top right. You will need approximately 17 inches (42 centimeters) of warp width to complete this project.

2. Using the scissors, cut 3 arm's-lengths of your white wool yarn. Using the tapestry needle, start weaving from left to right using the basic tabby weave. Weave 14 rows, or until you reach 6 centimeters high on the loom. On your 15 row, when you have reached the middle of the row, turn back to your starting point. On the next row, decrease the number of warp threads again. You might run out of yarn while doing this step; leave a 3-inch (7½-centimeter) tail every time you change to another thread. In the end, you will weave in all the tail ends.

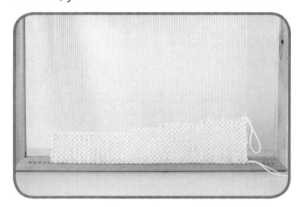

3. Change to the blue yarn and cut 2 arm's-lengths. Continue using tabby weave, applying the open slit technique each time your yarns meet in the middle of the loom (see instructions for open slit on page 29).

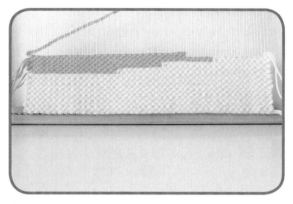

4. Now, to add a bit more texture to your piece, create a fringe with rya knots. Cut 70 strands of white yarn to 3 inches (7 centimeters) each. Make 14 rya knots, using 5 strands for each knot, on the right side of your loom (see instructions for rya knots page 26).

5. Grab the thick, bulky teal yarn, and cut 2 arm's-lengths. Start weaving on the left side of your loom using tabby weave. Work with your fingers instead of a needle; when you are working with really thick yarns, it's quicker if you use your hands to pass under and over the same way you do with tabby weave. Every time different yarns meet, do not interlock them, but use the open slit technique.

6. Using the white yarn again, first fill the unwoven space on the right and left sides of the teal yarn. Then weave 12 more rows, or until you are another 2 inches (5 centimeters) up the loom. Use your shed stick and shuttle to make this process easier. On the 13th row, when you reach the middle of the row, turn back to your starting point.

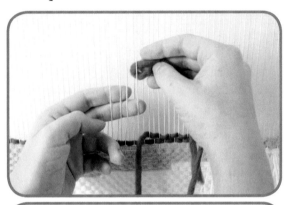

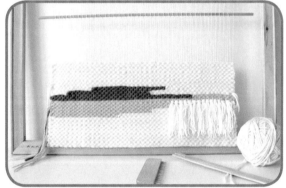

7. Change to the yellow yarn and weave an abstract shape on the right side of your loom. Then, switch to the thicker, bulky gray yarn to create texture, and weave another abstract shape in the middle of your woven piece. Don't worry if you can't replicate the exact patterns in these pictures; the beauty of this freeform weaving is that you can follow your own instinct and imagination.

8. Use the white yarn and fill the unwoven space around the yellow and gray yarns. Weave another 10 rows on top of that, or until you have woven 2 inches (5 centimeters) using the white yarn.

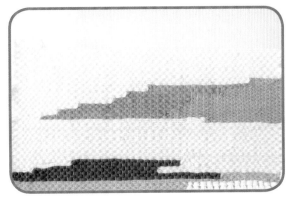

9. Cut 70 strands of white yarn to 3 inches (7 centimeters) each. Make 14 rya knots, using 5 strands for each knot, on the left side of your loom.

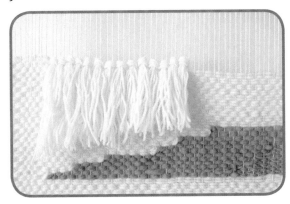

10. Start on the right side of your loom and add 5 rows of tabby weave using the black yarn. End your piece with a few more rows of the white yarn.

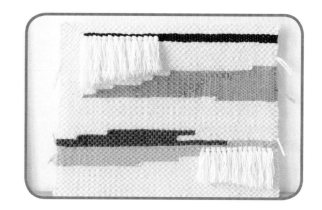

FINISHING STEPS:

11. Take your piece off the loom. Cut the top warp threads and tie them together in pairs. Unloop the bottom warp threads and leave them uncut. Adjust your weaving a bit toward the bottom, if needed.

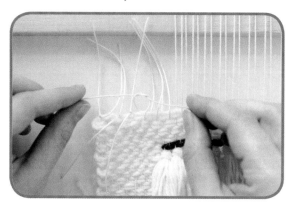

12. Weave your warp ends into the back of your piece, or if you prefer, tie them together. You don't need to have perfect finishings on this project because you won't see the back or the selvage of your piece in the completed version of the project.

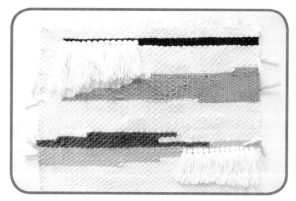

13. Cut a piece of fabric to the same size as your weaving. Pin the woven piece and the fabric together, with the front of the woven piece facing the fabric.

14. Sew them together, leaving an open space (approximately 6 inches, or 15¼ centimeters) to insert the stuffing. Turn the pillow inside out and stuff it. Sew the open gap using your needle and thread.

15. Display your new pillow in a favorite corner of your house.

MINIMALIST WALL HANGING

This wall hanging, as the name suggests, is an ode to minimalism. Embracing the philosophy "less is more," this piece is simple in form and color palette, and it is one of my favorites! In this project you will learn how to create a negative space, which means an open space on your weaving. Leaving areas free of weave is another element of interest you can add to your piece. Sometimes less is definitely more.

MATERIALS

* Weaving loom
* Cotton warp yarn
* Tapestry needle
* Lace weight single-ply wool yarn in black
* Worsted weight wool yarn in white
* Worsted weight two-ply cotton yarn in bronze
* Bulky weight yarn in black
* Scissors
* Weaving shuttle
* Shed stick
* Beater
* Approximately 14-inch (36-centimeter) wooden dowel

FINISHED SIZE: 14 x 20 inches (35 x 50 centimeters) including fringe

DIFFICULTY LEVEL:

INSTRUCTIONS:

1. Warp your loom starting with a double knot on the top left. Wrap your warp thread up and down the loom until you reach approximately 14 inches (35 centimeters) of warping width. Tie another double knot on the top right of your loom. You need to have approximately 14 inches (35 centimeters) of warping width. Check the tension on the warp after every turn on the loom.

2. Thread your tapestry needle with the black yarn. Now, start weaving 3 rows of tabby weave to support the fringe, which you will add next. Cut several strands of the black yarn to 11 inches (28 centimeters). You will need to make 31 rya knots, and the number of strands for each knot will depend on how thick your yarn is. Since my yarn was quite thin, I used 6 strands of yarn for each knot. Complete 1 row of rya knots. (See instructions for rya knots on page 26.)

3. Cut a length of the white yarn (approximately 2 yards), and fold it in half. Thread your needle with that yarn and start weaving on the right side of your loom. Weave 2 entire rows using tabby weave; on the third row, stop at the middle of your row and turn back. Repeat that process, decreasing the number of warp threads by 2 on each subsequent row (see instructions for diagonal slit on page 31). Stop when your last row has 12 warp threads. This will be the top of your figure.

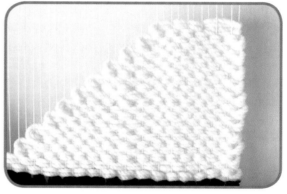

4. On the left side of your loom, repeat the exact same process you did in step 3. In the end, you will have woven 2 symmetrical diagonal figures and 1 empty upside down triangle in the middle.

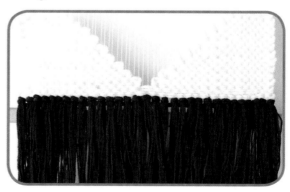

5. Prepare to make more rya knots. You can use the quick and easy technique to make rya knots that you have learned before in this book. Use the scissors to cut several strands of the white yarn to 6 inches (15 centimeters). You will need at least 5 strands for each knot to create a fluffy fringe if you are using a thin yarn like mine. Make 1 rya knot for every 2 warps, filling the space above the diagonal figure you just created.

6. Continue making rya knots until you fill all the spaces or finish 1 row. In the end, you will still have 1 empty triangle in the middle.

7. Continue using the white yarn. Cut 2 pieces of yarn approximately 2 arm's-lengths long. Make a knot on one end and use the 2 pieces of yarn to make 2 rows of soumak (see instructions for soumak on page 32).

8. In the place where you have your empty triangle, push the first row of soumak down gently with your fingers. This will help to lock the rya knots in place and prevent them from slipping into the negative space.

9. On top of your soumak, weave a few rows of tabby weave. Cut 1 yard of the white yarn, thread your needle, and start weaving from right to left. Use a shed stick and a shuttle to make this process quicker, since you are going to weave a large area (see instructions for using a shuttle on page 24). You might need to add more yarn several times to complete the space you need to weave. Leave at least a 4-inch (10-centimeter) tail every time you change yarn. In the end, weave all the tail ends into the back of your tapestry. Stop weaving when you are 2 inches (5 centimeters) up the loom.

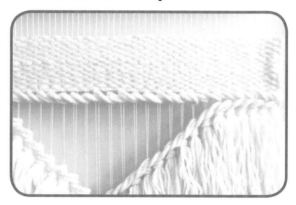

10. Change your yarn to a contrasting bronze color and weave 8 rows with tabby weave. Remember to use your tapestry beater to help you keep your weft tight, resulting in a more structured piece in the end.

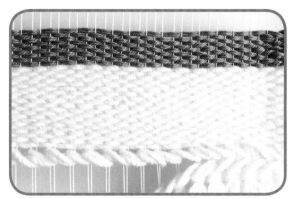

11. Change your yarn to a thicker, bulky black yarn. Weave 3 rows of tabby weave. Finish your tapestry with 2 rows of soumak using the same black yarn.

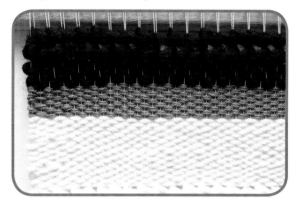

FINISHING STEPS:

12. Clean the back side of your piece by weaving in all the tail ends. Use a tapestry needle and stitch each yarn into the corresponding color area so it doesn't show on the front of your piece. Trim the excess.

13. Cut your bottom warps and tie them together in pairs. Be careful not to pull your knots too tight nor too loose; you need to apply the correct amount of tension so you don't affect the shape of you piece. Hide the warp ends on the back.

14. Unloop the top warp threads and leave them uncut. Insert your dowel through the loops, gently adjusting a few rows of weaving toward the top (see finishing instructions on page 36).

15. Cut a length of your cotton warp yarn and tie knots on each end of your dowel. Hang on a wall.

DRIFTWOOD BOARD

I live in a country where we have amazing beaches all over our coastline. I'm lucky enough to have my home just a few miles from the Atlantic Ocean, and I spend a lot of my time there, especially in the summer.

One of the things I like to do when I'm walking by the sea is look for unique seashells and old driftwood. Last summer, I found this beautiful rustic board.

This project is so, so simple, but adds a lot of character to this old driftwood. It's just another idea to give a new use to simple objects that you can find everywhere, or that you already have in your home.

MATERIALS

- Driftwood board
- Scissors
- Jute warp yarn
- Cotton yarns in multicolor, green, mint, teal, and beige
- Tapestry needle

FINISHED SIZE: 2½ x 13 inches (6 x 33 centimeters)

DIFFICULTY LEVEL: ✦✦✦✦✦✦

INSTRUCTIONS:

1. Go to the beach and look for a driftwood board. In this project, the driftwood board works as a natural loom. To warp your board, use the scissors to cut approximately 40 inches (101½ centimeters) of your jute yarn and wrap it around the board. Be careful to check the tension on your warp after each turn, or it will end up being too loose. Try to use the imperfections of your driftwood edges (top and bottom) to help you secure your warp in place.

2. Tie a double knot in the back of your board to secure the warps.

3. Cut a length of the multi-colored yarn and start weaving your board, approximately in the middle, using tabby weave. Be careful with the tension on your weft; don't push your yarn too much on the selvage edges (see instructions for tabby weave on page 23).

4. With the ocean and beach in mind, choose your color scheme. Select green and mint yarns to weave 2 diagonal shapes using tabby weave. To create your first diagonal shape in green, decrease the number of warp threads you use after each row, like you see in the photo. For the next diagonal shape in mint, use the opposite process and increase the number of warp threads as you weave. Use diagonal slit technique to join the 2 colors together (see instructions for diagonal slit on page 31).

5. Continue adding color by using a teal yarn. Weave another diagonal shape using tabby weave and leave an open space on the left side to create negative space. This is optional, but I thought it added another element of interest to my design. Finish the bottom part of your weaving with a few rows of tabby weave, again using the multicolored yarn.

6. Go to the other end of the board and add another diagonal shape using the beige yarn. Start creating the diagonal shape by using only the first warp thread and increase the number of warp threads as you weave up on the driftwood board.

7. Your woven driftwood board has a new and unique look. Embrace the imperfection of weaving on a natural piece.

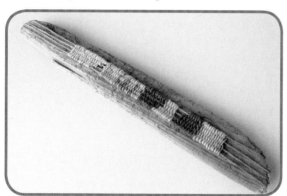

CIRCULAR WALL HANGING

This project is a whole new challenge even if you are a experienced weaver. Circular weaving is a new approach to weaving. You can use the same techniques you have already learned but you have to use them in a different way pushing you outside your comfort zone. I found it exciting and fun to experiment with circular weaving; hope you like it too!

MATERIALS

- ✤ Circular weaving loom
- ✤ Fine cotton warp yarn
- ✤ Wool and cotton yarns in peach, pink, coral, and white, white and coral bulky weight wool yarn, white wool roving
- ✤ Tapestry needle
- ✤ Scissors

Note: A circular weaving loom is, as the name suggests, a loom with a round shape and notches all around the outer edge of the circle. If you don't want to buy a circular loom like I did, you can make your own using a piece of round cardboard (the cheapest way) or use an embroidery hoop. Look on the Internet for more instructions on these options if you need to.

FINISHED SIZE: 10 inches x 20 inches (25 x 50 centimeters)

DIFFICULTY LEVEL:

INSTRUCTIONS:

1. Warp your circular loom. Using your warp thread, tie 1 double knot around 1 notch of the loom to secure the thread. Take the thread across the loom to the opposite notch.

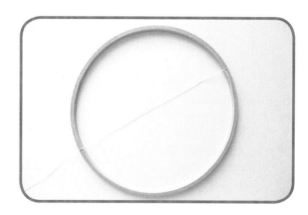

2. Wrap the thread around that notch and continue the same process backward and forward, going clockwise.

3. When you reach your starting point again, tie another double knot. The warp now has 2 levels. Use the top one to weave.

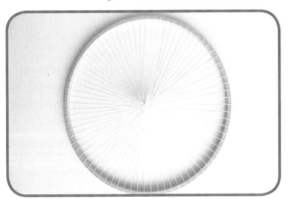

4. Start weaving in the center of your warping. Cut a length of the thin peach yarn to 25 inches (65 centimeters) and thread your tapestry needle with it. Weave under and over, like you do on tabby weave. Push the yarn to the center with your fingers or a needle. (If I start weaving with a thin thread, it's much easier, especially working with the overlapping of warp threads in the center. The thinner the yarn, the easier it is to get close to the center when weaving, and the better it will look in the end.) When you are weaving, do some bubbling with your yarn to avoid too much tension on the warp threads (see instructions for bubbling on page 26).

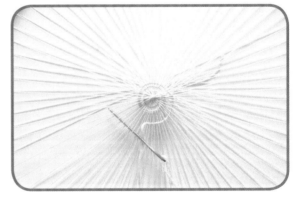

5. Change to the pink yarn, cut 20 inches (50 centimeters), and continue weaving around the center. Every time you start with a new yarn, you must interlock the 2 yarns together. In order to do that, you must pull the new strand of yarn through the loop created by the first yarn, so they will share the same warp thread and become attached together (see instructions for weft interlocking on page 29).

6. Switch to the thicker, bulky white yarn and weave 3 rows of tabby weave. For that, you will need a strand of yarn 30 inches (80 centimeters) long. Since this yarn is a bit thick and the warps are very close to each other, I recommend going under and over 2 warp threads at a time.

7. Change to the thinner coral yarn. Cut 1 yard and continue weaving around the loom using tabby weave. Remember to interlock your yarns every time you change from one to the other.

8. Weave a few rows using different yarns to create contrast on your piece. Use tabby weave technique to weave with each yarn. To create a more asymmetrical effect, like the one I created with this piece, don't always end your yarns in the same place. When you end one yarn and start a new one, try to do so on opposite sides of your loom. Remember to pack your yarn with a beater after each turn; that creates a more structured piece.

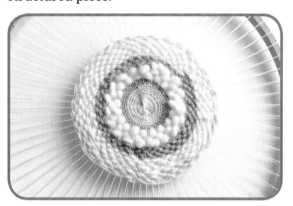

9. Choose one thick yarn, like the bulky wool yarn in coral, and start weaving a row of soumak (see instructions for soumak on page 32). For this you will need approximately 50 inches (120 centimeters) of bulky yarn. Complete one entire row. Soumak will add another element of texture and movement to your piece.

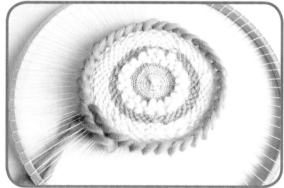

10. Weave an entire row using white wool roving. You will need at least 1 yard of that yarn to complete 1 row. To weave with roving, you need to pass your yarn under the first warp thread and over the next 2 warps, then again under 1 warp and over 2, and continue repeating that method until you reach the end of the row. To add a "bubble" effect, in the spaces where you weaved over 2 warps, gently push the yarn up just a little. Be careful not to push too much on your roving yarn because it can affect the shape of your piece once you take it off the loom.

11. Weave the final 3 or 4 rows of tabby weave around the roving yarn using white wool yarn.

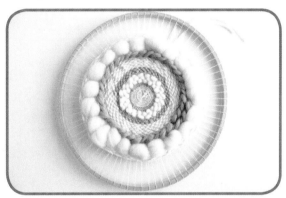

FINISHING STEPS:

12. To finish your piece, cut the warp threads on the back of your loom in the middle. Knot the ends together 2 at a time. Sew them into the back of your weaving with a needle.

13. Add some rya knots on one side to work as fringe. Add a piece of yarn on top to hang your new work of art.

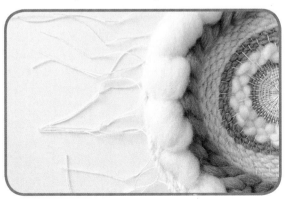

HANGING PLANTER

I'm a plant addict. My home is always full of plants. I like how they bring life and color to my home. My favorites are the hanging plants, and making this woven plant hanger was also an excuse to buy another one!

MATERIALS

- Cardboard
- Small pot
- Masking tape
- Resistant, 100% cotton warp thread
- Wool yarn in white and green
- Scissors
- 2 tapestry needles, one larger than the other
- Tapestry beater

FINISHED SIZE: 40 x 5 inches (101½ x 12½ cm)

DIFFICULTY LEVEL:

INSTRUCTIONS:

1. Using the scissors, cut a piece of cardboard the same size as the top circumference of your pot. Stick the cardboard around the pot with masking tape. Wrap your thread around the outside of your pot. Start by tying a double knot at the top. Carry your warp thread across the top and bottom of the pot, creating your warp. This will be your loom.

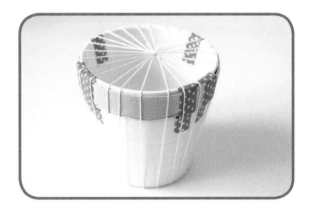

2. Prepare to make a fringe for your hanging pot. Cut several pieces of green yarn to 7 inches (18 centimeters). Make rya knots all around the bottom of your pot using 3 lengths of yarn for each knot (see instructions for rya knots on page 26).

3. On top of your rya knots, weave a few rows with tabby weave. Weave under and over every warp thread using the 2 strands of white yarn. For this, use a needle with a larger hole. Every time you have to change your yarn, leave a 3-inch (7½-centimeter) tail that you will hide in the end.

4. Change back to a contrasting green yarn and weave a few rows using tabby weave. Switch to your white yarn again and continue weaving all the way to the top. Be sure to keep the weaving tight; you will need a sturdy support for your vase. For this, use your tapestry beater. Play with more colors or add more fringe to your plant hanger if you feel this is too simple for you.

5. When you finish your weaving, cut the threads on top and tie them together 2 at a time. Cut 3 lengths of yarn to 50 inches (130 centimeters) and fold them in half. Weave each of them to the pot. In the end, you will have 3 sets of 2 cords all the same length. Add a beautiful plant and display it in a window of your home.